Hats

Hats

STEWART, TABORI & CHANG

NEW YORK

FUNCTION VS. STYLE

**Virtue may
flourish in an
old cravat,
but man and
nature scorn
the shocking hat.**

Oliver Wendell Holmes

Her hat—oh, it was romance, it was mystery, it was strange, sweet sorrow...

Dorothy Parker

"Don't you like this hat?"

"No, sir."

"Well I do," I replied rather cleverly, and went out with it tilted just that merest shade over the left eye which makes all the difference.

P. G. WODEHOUSE

I have recently acquired a new hat of such ferocity that it has been running my whole life for me. I wake up in the morning thinking *who shall I wear my hat at today?*

KATHARINE WHITEHORN

...a woman's hat is close to her heart, though she wears it on her head. It is her way of saying to the world: See this is what I am like—or this is what I would like to be.

Lilly Daché

A little bad taste is like a nice splash of paprika. Diana Vreeland

Her hat is a creation that will never go out of style. It will look just as ridiculous year after year. FRED ALLEN

HAT BOX

WORK / STRE

NGTH/FORM

It was astonishing how fashionable it was to be unfaithful. He often wondered if it had anything to do with going without a hat. No sooner had the homburgs and the bowlers disappeared from the City than everyone grew their hair longer, and after that nothing was sacred. BERYL BAINBRIDGE

Every style of hat is identified with some form of undesirable (derby = corrupt ward heeler; fedora = Italian gangster; top hat = rich bum; pillbox = Kennedy wife, et cetera).

P J O'Rourke

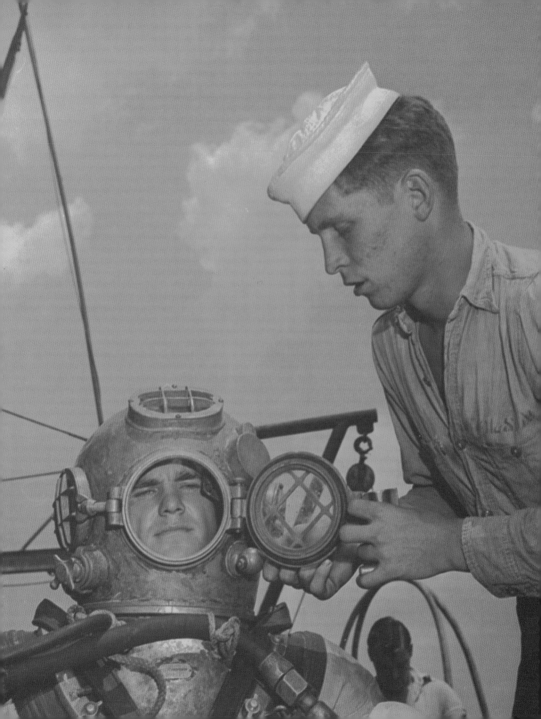

Beware of all enterprises that require new clothes.

HENRY DAVID THOREAU

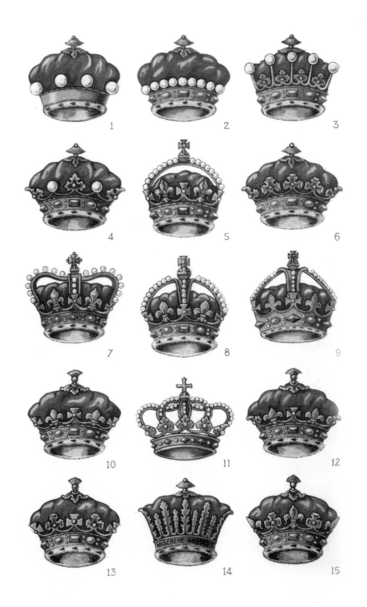

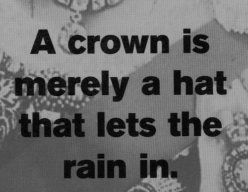

A crown is merely a hat that lets the rain in.

Frederick The Great,
King of Prussia

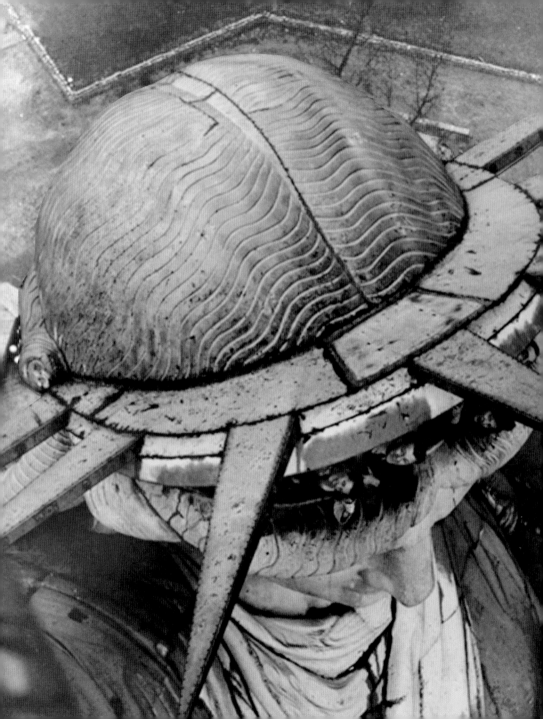

Fashion is architecture:
it is a matter of
proportions.
Coco Chanel

33

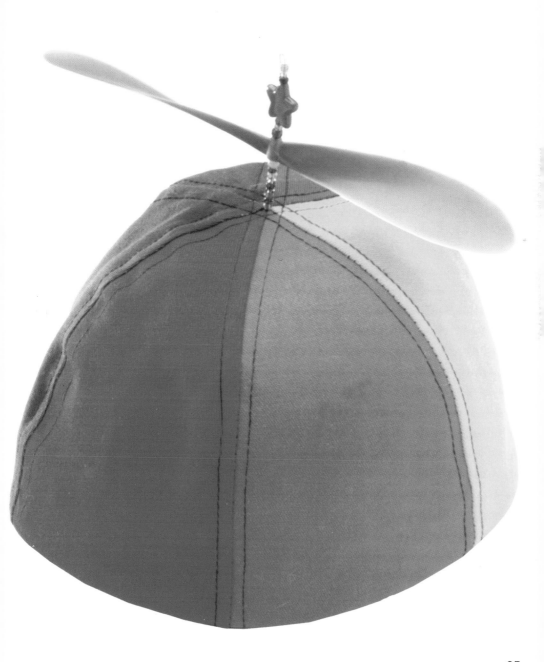

All good hats are made out of nothing.

Oscar Wilde

"There is not so variable a thing in nature as a lady's head-dress"

JOSEPH ADDISON

...she's only got two ideas in her head. The other one's hats.

ERIC LINKLATER

He can't think
without his hat.

Samuel Beckett

The rush of power to the head
is not as becoming
as a new hat.

Helen Van Slyke

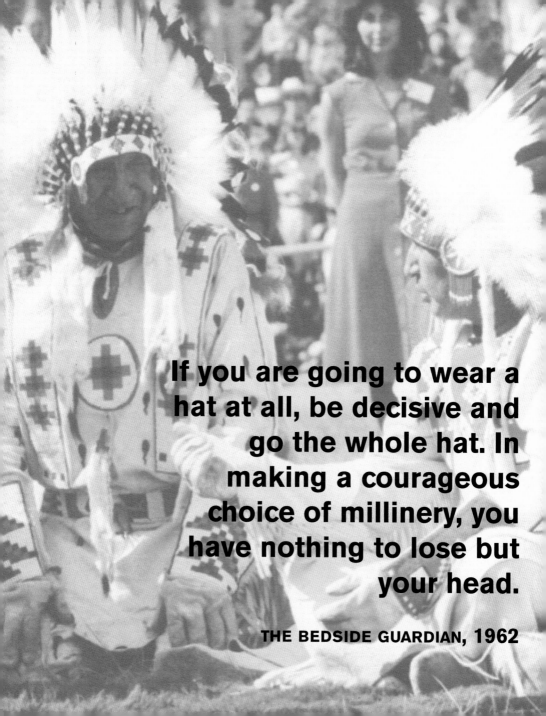

If you are going to wear a hat at all, be decisive and go the whole hat. In making a courageous choice of millinery, you have nothing to lose but your head.

THE BEDSIDE GUARDIAN, 1962

When he had to leave for his train, there were no clinging farewells, no tender words to keep. He had gone to the door and opened it and stood with it against his shoulder while he shook out his flight cap and put it on, adjusting it with great care, one inch over the eye, one inch above the ear. She stood in the middle of the living-room, cool and silent, looking at him. When his cap was precisely as it should be he looked at her.

DOROTHY PARKER, *THE LOVELY LEAVE*

HAT TRICK

ICON

I never take my hat off in public.

Frank Sinatra

"Whaddya rebellin' against, Joh___?"

"Wha' ya go___

Marlon Brando ___e Wild One

Style is knowing who you are, what you want to say, and not giving a damn.

Gore Vidal

Fashion is a kind of communication. It's a language without words.

HELMUT LANG

Some men's hats are as easily blown away as their heads.

George Savile, Marquis of Halifax

It isn't what I do,
but how I do it. It
isn't what I say, but
how I say it, and
how I look when I
do it and say it.

MAE WEST

There he adjusted his hat with care, and regarded himself very seriously, very sternly, from various angles, like a man invited to paint his own portrait for the Uffizi.

MAX BEERBOHM

HAT BAND

ACTIVE HAT

$H^{AT}_{2}O$

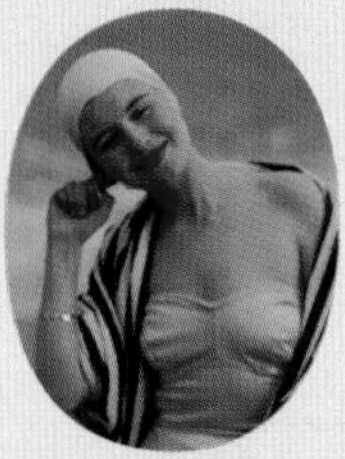

putting on the

ritz

HATS OFF

TO...

Picture Credits

page 4/5: Carmen Miranda, circa 1945.

page 7: Cecil Beaton and one of the Ascot cosumes he designed for the film *My Fair Lady*, 1971.

page 8: Corkscrew headdress, circa 1955.

page 9: Clockwise from top right, Victor Jay cloche hat, circa 1928; cloche hat, 1929; Victor Jay cloche hat, circa 1928; cloche hat, 1927.

page 10: Ernie Kovaks, 1962.

page 12: Dame Edith Sitwell, 1962.

page 14: Vivien Leigh in the title role of the film *Anna Karenina*, 1948.

page 15: From top to bottom, Brigitte Bardot, 1967; Jacqueline Kennedy, 1960; Sophia Loren, 1965.

page 16: Red feather hat, 1956.

page 19: Hedda Hopper, 1961.

page 20/21: Julie Andrews in the film *Thoroughly Modern Millie*, 1966.

page 22/23: British policemen modeling the new style of helmet (left), issued for picket and riot duties, 1977.

page 26: From left to right, Edward Woods in the film *Public Enemy*, 1931; Humphrey Bogart, 1951; C. Henry Gordon in the film *Scarface*, 1932.

page 27: Al Capone, circa 1930.

page 28: Diving suit, US Navy Salvage School, Bayonne, New Jersey, 1955.

page 29: From top to bottom, RAF pilot wearing a high altitude helmet, 1955; Yuri Gagarin, 1961; American football player wearing a padded head protector, 1940.

page 31: Queen Victoria.

page 32/33: The Statue of Liberty, New York, 1930.

page 37: Marcel Marceau, Sadler's Wells Theatre, London, 1972.

page 38: Clockwise from top right, Easter bonnet, designed by Rose Bertin, 1943; Twiggy, circa 1962; Joanna Lumley, 1966.

page 39: Barbra Streisand in the film *Hello Dolly,* 1963, Ernst Haas/Hulton Getty.

page 40: Dancer in feathered headdress, 1965.

page 42: Ernesto Che Guevara, 1965.

page 43: Clockwise from top right, Fidel Castro, 1987, Paul O'Driscoll, The Observer/Hulton Getty; Mao Tse-Tung, 1976; Josef Stalin, 1931; Vladimir Ilyich Lenin, circa 1922.

page 44: Mobutu Sese Seko (Joseph Desire Mobutu), 1978.

page 46/47: Prince Charles with Native American leaders, Canada, 1975.

page 50/51: Paul Daniels, 1980.

page 52/53: James Dean in the film *Giant*, 1955.

page 54: Frank Sinatra, 1958.

page 56/57: Marlon Brando in the film *The Wild One,* 1954.

page 58: John Wayne, circa 1939

page 61: Marlene Dietrich, 1935.

page 62/63: Jimi Hendrix, 1967.

page 63: From top to bottom, Marc Bolan, 1972; Lou Reed, 1976.

page 65: Mae West, circa 1932.

page 66/67: Woody Allen, 1975, Peter Gould, Images/Hulton Getty.

page 68/69: The Beatles, 1963.

page 70/71: Lester Piggott, 1966.

page 73: Swimming hats, 1954.

page 74: Fred Astaire, 1946.

page 75: From left to right, Constance Cummings in the film *Broadway Thru a Keyhole,* 1933; Marlene Dietrich, 1930.

page 76/77: Graduating Cadets, US Air Force Academy, Colorado, 1966.

Published in 1999 by
Stewart, Tabori & Chang
A division of U.S. Media Holdings, Inc.
115 West 18th Street
New York, NY 10011

Distributed in Canada by
General Publishing Company Ltd.
30 Lesmill Road
Don Mills, Ontario, Canada M3B 2T6

Library of Congresss Catalog Card Number: 98-88625

ISBN: 1-55670-887-4

Design concept: Senate
Additional design: John Casey
Series Editor: Elizabeth Cotton
Printed in Italy

10 9 8 7 6 5 4 3 2 1